Cleaning Up Our Wetland

Written by Anna Porter

Photography by Michael Curtain

Flying Start
to Literacy®

Contents

What a mess!

The wetland near our school was a mess. It was full of rubbish and the water was polluted.

Our teacher told us that the wetland used to have lots of birds in it. Many of the birds left the wetland when it became polluted.

We decided to clean up our wetland.

Week 1

First, we had to pull out lots of weeds.
We put these weeds into a big bag.
We had them taken away so they would
not spread their seeds into the wetland.

Then we picked up all the rubbish.
We sorted it, put it in big bags
and had it taken away.

We took a sample of water from the
wetland and put it in a jar. We had
the water tested to see how polluted
it was.

Week 2

What do we want?

We wanted the birds to come back to the wetland, so we found out what these birds need for food and for their habitat.

We found out that ducks need to eat water plants. We found out that some birds, like pelicans, need to rest in big trees. These birds use reeds from the water to make their nests.

Week 1

Week 2

Week 3

We also found out that swans use reeds to make their nests on top of the water. They like to dive under the water to dig up the roots of plants to eat.

We hoped that when the wetland was clean, frogs and other insects would come back to it. The birds in the wetland eat these animals.

Week 1

Week 2

Week 3

Week 4

A lot of work!

We selected plants that we knew the birds and other animals would like to feed on or shelter in. Then we took these plants to the wetland.

We dug holes for the plants. We put on rubber boots and gloves. We put the plants in the holes and tied them to sticks so that the plants would stand up.

Week 1　　　Week 2　　　Week 3　　　Week 4

Week 5

We planted water lilies in the shallow water.

We planted reeds close to the water on the banks of the wetland.

We planted some grasses and small bushes that would have lots of flowers around the edge of the wetland.

Week 1

Week 2

Week 3

Week 4

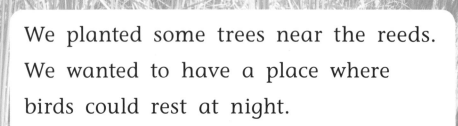

We planted some trees near the reeds. We wanted to have a place where birds could rest at night.

We hoped that the pelicans would come back to the wetland.
We hoped that the swans would use the reeds to make nests in the middle of the water.

Week 1

Week 2

Week 3

Week 4

Week 5

Week 6

Week 7

We put up labels with the names of the plants on them.

Then we took photos of the plants and the wetland and we checked these photos against the photos of the polluted wetland.

We also took new samples of water to see how much cleaner the water had become. We did this to check how much the wetland had changed.

Week 1   Week 2   Week 3   Week 4

Week 5

Week 6

Week 7

Getting the news out

Then we made a poster to explain how we had cleaned up the wetland. The poster said which plants we had chosen for the wetland and why we had chosen them.

The poster also asked people not to feed the birds at the wetland as they now had lots of plants to eat.

Week 1   Week 2   Week 3   Week 4

Week 5

Week 6

Week 7

Week 8

Our wetland looks so much better now. We can't wait to see which birds will come back to live in it.

A note from the author

This book is based on what a group of children did in a wetland near where I live. I used to go and watch them as they worked hard to clear up the wetland and replant the types of plants that would provide shelter for the animals or food for them to eat.

I loved to see all the birds returning to the wetland. I kept notes of what the children did each week in my journal, so I thought the calendar was a good idea to show their efforts over time.